THE
BUSINESS OWNER'S
FREEDOM
FLYWHEEL

MAKE YOUR BUSINESS
FUN TO **RUN** (NOW)
AND **EASY** TO **SELL** (LATER)

DAWN BLOOMER

THE
BUSINESS OWNER'S
FREEDOM
FLYWHEEL

MAKE YOUR BUSINESS
FUN TO **RUN** (NOW)
AND **EASY** TO **SELL** (LATER)

DAWN BLOOMER

SPECIAL INVITATION

Be sure to get all of the bonuses
included in this book.

You'll find them at:

ProductivePressure.com/Flywheel

*To my dad—who always had the best advice,
whether I was ready to hear it or not.*

*When you retired, you said,
"I have enough money
to do everything I ever wanted…
I'm just not sure I have enough time left."*

*I love you for teaching me
how to think, lead, and live.*

*This book is for business owners who want to build
something great without missing out along the
way—who want freedom now, not just someday.*

Notes.

HOW TO USE THIS BOOKMARK:

1. JOT DOWN IDEAS.

2. NOTE WHAT YOU'D LIKE TO WORK ON WITH YOUR COACH.

3. CAPTURE ACTION ITEMS THAT NEED YOUR ATTENTION!

THANKS FOR READING!

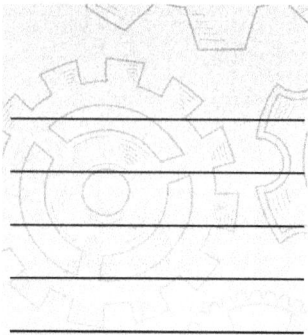

TABLE OF CONTENTS

INTRODUCTION

Entrepreneurs are wired differently.

We wear overcommitment like a badge of honor. We're addicted to solving problems, chasing growth, and proving we can do more—*because we can.*

We thrive on the challenge, the hustle, and the satisfaction of making it work. But what happens when the very qualities that drive us forward also start to hold us back?

Many entrepreneurs have been there. They start their journey with a grand vision and unlimited energy. But then the excitement fades and they wind up feeling worn out instead of inspired.

I was no different.

As a veterinarian for racehorses, my truck was my office, my pharmacy, and sometimes even my bedroom. I worked six to seven days a week, was on call 24/7, and I *loved* it.

The drive. The responsibility. The process of figuring everything out. It was *fun*.

When I became a mom, I was determined to prove I could handle it all: the demanding career, the business with its constant demands, and parenting. My newborn son, Jack, spent his days either in the truck with me and our nanny or in a makeshift nursery I'd set up in a tack room in one of the barns. At the time, I thought it was a pretty clever solution—a way to keep him close without sacrificing my clients' needs or my business goals.

Running a business and working full time as a veterinarian wasn't easy. My clients counted on me for everything—calling at all hours with emergencies or questions they didn't trust anyone else with.

My team looked to me to solve problems and give them support. But no matter how much I did, I always felt like I was dropping the ball on something.

I didn't want to miss a moment with Jack, either, but that meant toting him around everywhere. Balancing work and motherhood felt like juggling flaming torches while riding a unicycle.

By the time my daughter, Emma, came along, I took it a step further. I bought an RV, parked it at the racetrack, and made it their home away from home. It gave the kids—and the nanny—more space, a bathroom, and some of the comforts of home.

They were still close to me while I worked. But it also created some additional effort because it meant stocking diapers, bottles, clothes, and supplies in the truck, the RV, and the barn nursery.

I kept telling myself, *These are first-world problems, right? Just make it work.*

And I *did*. Until I couldn't.

One day, I found myself hiding in a too-small barn bathroom stall with my knees pressed against the door, desperate for just five minutes to think.

People were always banging on my truck window, opening the door to ask me a question while I was trying to cram some food in my mouth, or calling me at all hours of the day or night to ask something that just couldn't wait.

But in that tiny bathroom, with its low, jockey-size doors, I could finally escape.

Sitting there, I realized I'd spent years *adding*—piling on more responsibilities, more pressure, more expectations—without stopping to ask whether I *should*. I had the title, the "success," the income, and the respect of my clients and peers. All the things a business owner wants.

But I didn't have the one thing I desperately needed most: *freedom*.

MY "WHY" CHANGED

That moment marked the start of a shift. I knew I couldn't keep going the way I had been. I needed to redefine what success looked like for me and figure out how to make our business *work for me*, not the other way around. What I experienced that day wasn't about burnout—it was about the realization that success without intention isn't true success. The same traits that helped make our business successful—drive, resilience, and the ability to solve problems— were also trapping me.

In the early days of our practice, the way I got traction with clients was to be available to everybody, all the time. If you called me, I would pick up the phone no matter what time of the day or night it was.

I tolerated people texting me in the evening or calling me on my day off. I'm not proud to admit this, but the day after I gave birth to Emma, I was on the phone talking to a client about what they needed to do with their horse. (You know how it is with the second child, right?)

As one of my mentors once said, "You teach the behavior you tolerate!"

I taught my coworkers and clients that I was always available and that they needed me for everything. I said yes to every opportunity and every challenge.

I didn't think there was anything wrong with this at the time, though. I thought being available 24/7 was just part of being a successful business owner. You're busy. You're in demand. You do what it takes to make people happy and serve them well.

But somewhere along the way, it stopped feeling good. My priorities had shifted, but I'd been too busy to notice.

When I first started out, I was single. All I wanted was to be a great veterinarian. I wanted to own a business, make lots of money, and have all of the things I'd ever dreamed of.

Later, when I got married and started having kids, I also wanted to be a good spouse and parent. Like a lot of business owners who also happen to have responsibilities outside of work, I realized that I wanted more from life than just to be a great veterinarian.

My *why* had changed.

That happens to most of us because we almost never stop to reevaluate what really matters to us. It's a huge problem for business owners because we're so busy, we don't take time to pause and think about the deeper questions.

Why am I doing this? What do I want to get out of it? What kind of life do I want my business to support? And why do I want it?

Spoiler alert: If you don't figure it out, you might end up with a business you don't even like anymore.

For me, the wake-up call was realizing that my business wasn't working for me—in fact, the opposite was true. But once I got clear on what I wanted and *why*, I started looking at how my business could give me freedom and options, not just money.

> **ONCE YOU KNOW WHAT YOU WANT AND WHY YOU WANT IT, THE REST IS JUST LOGISTICS.**

FROM VET TO BUSINESS & EXIT STRATEGIST

I don't want to give the impression that just because I had a light bulb moment of clarity, things immediately turned around. Far from it. To run my business smarter instead of harder required learning—a lot of learning.

In fact, my transition from veterinarian to Business & Exit Strategist wasn't one of those cool and inspiring social media–worthy success stories. It was more like a shitshow involving a lot of mistakes, faceplants, and moments of sheer panic.

As my partners and I grew our practice, by necessity I became more involved in the business side of things. I realized I really enjoyed that part, but I also didn't have any formal business training. I was really good at being a veterinarian, but business? Was I really doing the right things?

After all, I'd become an entrepreneur by accident. So, I decided to do what I knew had worked for me in the past—get a degree. I took classes and got my MBA online while continuing to do everything else.

While I wouldn't recommend my approach to anyone, my studies did help me realize that our business needed to change if we wanted it to survive long term. There were external forces at play, such as regulatory changes and other economic factors, that we couldn't control but needed to anticipate.

We also had internal challenges, such as associates who weren't that interested in business ownership, that would affect how we could eventually exit the business.

Not to mention, our financials had been neglected, vendor pricing had not been renegotiated, and we'd never updated any of our operating agreements (even after the departure of some partners). The list went on and on.

In the short term, I knew I needed to find ways to stop being a bottleneck. In the long term, we needed a way to eventually transfer ownership if we wanted to get any real value from our sweat equity.

I focused on turning our business into the cash cow it could be—without needing me or my partner for its continued success. We needed systems and processes, more leadership depth, and a way to build value that didn't require us to be at the center of things.

Once we got our business working properly and I stopped micromanaging everything—more on that later—we were able to explore options for transitioning ownership.

We eventually merged our practice with a group of other practices, where I had the opportunity to help acquire more veterinary practices. As part of this process, I met with many owners who wanted to sell their businesses, and those conversations were eye-opening.

Most of the businesses I evaluated weren't sellable—not because they weren't profitable, but because they were completely dependent on the owner. They were lifestyle businesses, designed to fund their owners' day-to-day lives, but without any systems, leadership depth, or transferable value.

It broke my heart to explain to these owners that the business they had poured their blood, sweat, and tears into—their "baby"—was worth little more than the value of its assets minus its liabilities.

They had essentially built themselves a very well-paying job, one that no one else could take over because it was too reliant on them. I hated having those conversations, but it opened my eyes to how widespread the problem is.

> STATISTICS SHOW THAT ONLY AROUND 20 PERCENT TO 30 PERCENT OF BUSINESSES THAT GO TO MARKET ARE SUCCESSFULLY SOLD.[1]

As a result, I started asking myself: *How can I help other business owners avoid these mistakes? How do I show them how to build something that's fun to run now and easy to sell later?*

---

1 https://www.forbes.com/sites/forbesfinancecouncil/2023/08/24/business-exit-planning-watch-for-these-blind-spots/

Those same questions were on my mind as I wrote *The Business Owner's Freedom Flywheel.*

You may have picked up this book because you know your business isn't as fun to run as it could be, and you're dreading getting it ready to sell when the time comes.

Please know that not only have I been where you are, I can help you get to where you want to go.

But before we get into the details of the Freedom Flywheel, I want to take a few moments in Chapter One to share a critical message you need to hear as we begin this journey: You can do this!

You Can
Do This!

YOU CAN DO THIS!

If there's one thing I know about you, it's this: You didn't achieve this level of success by accident.

You've earned every inch of progress with grit, determination, and probably more coffee than you'd like to admit. Sure, there were wins, a few lessons disguised as challenges, and maybe even a leap of faith or two that made your stomach drop.

But here you are.

And no matter how many plates you've got spinning in the air right now, you've got this. You can absolutely create a business that works for you—without feeling like it's calling the shots.

As a business owner, you signed up for the excitement of running your own show. But you also have to admit that it's a lot, always being the person everyone comes to.

When you're that busy, it can be hard to picture what might be possible. But just for a few moments, take yourself out of the day-to-day world of your business and dream.

LET'S IMAGINE SOMETHING DIFFERENT

Imagine this: Your alarm goes off in the morning, and instead of hitting snooze three times, you're actually excited to get out of bed.

I know, wild concept, right? But stay with me. You don't feel like you're walking into yet another day of putting out fires. You're not already bracing yourself for the fifteenth email labeled "URGENT" before you've had your coffee.

Instead, you wake up energized—maybe even happy—because your business doesn't just function; it flows.

You've got a team that actually runs like the well-oiled machine you always dreamed of, which means you're no longer holding the operation together with duct tape and sheer willpower.

Customers? They're not just satisfied; they're thrilled, and their drama-free energy actually makes your day better.

And here's the kicker: Financially, you're killing it. Bills? Paid. Profits? Growing. Retirement? It's no longer a dream. You're living the life you've worked so hard for and planning for a future that excites you.

Oh, and let's add this little cherry on top: If someone knocked on your door and offered to buy your business tomorrow, you wouldn't be scrambling to pull it together. You'd be ready—calm, confident, and ready to say "yes" on *your* terms.

Sounds like a pipe dream? It's not. This dream is absolutely within reach. You're not here because your business is failing. You're here because you want it to be better.

And that's exactly what we're going to accomplish together.

But don't just take my word for it. Let me introduce you to a couple of business owners who had every appearance of success on the outside but were secretly stuck in the hamster wheel of busy. They made the leap from running on fumes to running their business with freedom and intention.

If they can do it, so can you.

THE ARCHITECT WHO WAS THE BOTTLENECK

One of my clients was an architect who seemed to have it all together—on the surface.

He loved his work, drove a nice car, and lived in a beautiful neighborhood. But behind the scenes, things were not as they seemed. He hadn't saved enough for his future, his business wasn't set up to be sellable, and—big surprise—everything had to go through him.

Every decision, every approval—he was the Grand Central Station of his own company. And yes, he knew he was the bottleneck, but he had no idea how to fix it.

His accounts receivable was a mess, and there wasn't a plan for what would happen when he was ready to step away.

We started by clarifying his long-term goals and mapping out a plan to increase the value of his business. Then came the hard part: delegation. Slowly but surely, he began handing off tasks, trusting his team, and building systems that didn't involve him being in the middle of everything.

The payoff? He finally took those RV trips he'd been dreaming about, started saving for his future, and even began exploring potential buyers for his business. For the first time, his business supported his life instead of running it.

THE CASH-PRINTING BUSINESS WITHOUT A PLAN

Then there were the partners in a wildly profitable business. On paper, everything looked amazing—they were practically printing money. But there was one big problem: They didn't have an exit strategy.

They realized that if they didn't figure it out, they might have to just shut things down one day and walk away from years of hard work (and cash flow).

We worked together to get their operations running like clockwork, documented the value of their business, and positioned it for a sale. The result? They didn't just save their business—they sold it for more than they ever expected to.

These clients weren't billionaires with unlimited resources. They were regular business owners who decided they were done with the chaos and ready for a change.

And guess what? If they could do it, so can you.

Before we get into the details of how you can make this happen in your own business, let's take a quick look at three important questions— Why me?, Why you?, and Why now?—and then we will explore what the Freedom Flywheel is all about.

WHY ME?

You might wonder why I'm even the right person to bring you this message. After all, I didn't get it all right the first time around. In fact, I made a lot of mistakes.

Those mistakes are precisely what make me uniquely qualified to write this book.

> **FOR YEARS, I WAS SO BUSY WORKING *IN* MY BUSINESS THAT I DIDN'T WORK *ON* IT. THE MONEY KEPT COMING IN, AND I THOUGHT THAT WAS ENOUGH.**

Then the market crash of 2008 hit, and I realized working harder wasn't going to solve the problem. I had to work smarter.

I also learned the hard way about the importance of planning for an exit. While we eventually sold to a larger aggregator, I know that if I'd started planning earlier, I could have secured better terms and more value.

My experiences as a business owner, buyer, seller, and strategist shaped the Freedom Flywheel framework you're about to learn.

WHY YOU?

This book is for business owners who want more—more profit, more freedom, and more time to focus on what really matters.

If you're someone who:

- takes action and responsibility for your success
- dreams bigger but wants strategic growth—not growth for growth's sake

- is willing to learn from mistakes and adapt to new strategies

- is overwhelmed by the day-to-day grind and wants less stress and more freedom, and

- wants to run a business, not let it run their life

… then you're in the right place!

Now, you might be thinking, *This sounds great for someone running a big, fancy business, but what about me?* I get it. Not everyone fits the same mold, and that's okay.

Whether you're the owner of a business knocking on the door of $5 million, you've consistently been hitting $10 million, or you're almost to $50 million, this book can help. And I just might be the person you've been looking for!

Here is just a sampling of what you'll learn in the pages ahead:

- How to take more time off without worrying your business will collapse the second you step away.

- How to reduce stress, free up time in your day-to-day, and actually grow—even if you already feel like you're running on fumes.

- Practical, doable ways to make your business more efficient, profitable, and less of a constant headache.

This isn't about adding more to your already full plate—it's about clearing some space so you can actually enjoy what you're building. Wherever you're starting from, this framework will help you to create a business that works for you, not the other way around.

WHY NOW?

Let me share a few simple business realities that make this book urgently needed.

The first reality, as I mentioned earlier, is you *will* exit your business someday. You may do it vertically or horizontally. But there is a 100 percent chance it will happen.

In fact, there are five common reasons people exit their business unexpectedly. We call them the "5 Ds":

- Death,
- Disability,
- Divorce (being forced to sell your business),
- Disagreement (partnership disagreements are very common), and
- Distress (due to market conditions, regulatory changes, or elements beyond your control).

If you don't have a plan, your business may not survive your departure, let alone have any value.

The second business reality is that many entrepreneurs believe they can't get away from their business for any length of time because they're afraid it will fall apart.

Without the right team and structure in place, the owner wears all the hats in the company. They often struggle to take time off, let alone take a real vacation. A study published in the *Harvard Business Review* showed that 96 percent of U.S. professionals say they need flexibility, but only 47 percent actually have it.[1]

Let's be honest. Even if you love your work, you need to have space for the other aspects of your life. You need better systems so you can breathe and enjoy the life you deserve.

And the third business reality is that just 30 percent of family businesses make it to the second generation, and the numbers decrease with each generation.[2] So if you're thinking of passing your business on to the next generation—perhaps a family member or a long-term employee—start planning now.

---

1 https://hbr.org/2018/06/96-of-u-s-professionals-say-they-need-flexibility-but-only-47-have-it

2 https://www.im-financial.com/blog/the-generational-decline-why-success-becomes-harder-with-each-generation-i

> **THE SOONER YOU START PLANNING, THE MORE OPTIONS YOU'LL HAVE— AND THE MORE LIKELY YOUR BUSINESS WILL GIVE YOU THE LIFE YOU WANT, BOTH *NOW* AND *LATER*.**

What can you do to avoid the pitfalls that trip up so many owners? I'm so glad you asked.

THE FREEDOM FLYWHEEL

The Freedom Flywheel is a simple, actionable framework designed to help you build a business that's fun to run now and easy to sell later.

The concept of a flywheel is powerful: It builds momentum over time, becomes self-sustaining, and keeps turning with less effort. In this same way, each of the seven elements of the Freedom Flywheel builds on the last, creating energy and progress.

Here is an overview, and I promise we'll dive deeply into each element in the chapters to come:

- *Fix the Fires:* Remove the obstacles slowing you down.

- *Reverse Engineer Your Plan:* Define your destination and work backward.

- *Embrace Metrics That Matter:* Focus on what truly drives success.

- *Establish Owner Independence:* Build systems and leadership so your business can run without you.

- *Drive Growth and Scalability:* Expand strategically for long-term impact.

- *Optimize Profitability:* Ensure every effort maximizes results.

- *Multiply Your Value:* Position your business as a scalable, sellable asset.

This isn't just theory—it's a methodology grounded in practical, tested strategies from someone who's been in the trenches. And it's not about someday off in the unforeseeable future. It's about building a business that works for you *now*.

In the next chapter, we'll tackle the fires stealing your time and energy. You'll learn how to create space to breathe, focus, and regain control, and best of all, you'll stop having to put out the same flames over and over again.

Let's get started. Your future, chaos-free business awaits!

Fix the
Fires

CHAPTER TWO

FIX THE FIRES

In your imagination, picture a boardroom full of a company's leaders. They're dissecting a spreadsheet projected onto the big-screen TV and debating projections like their lives depend on it. The tension is palpable.

Meanwhile, the office next to them is burning. Smoke is billowing out the door and seeping through the air vents. Huge orange flames are visibly licking at the glass doors of the boardroom.

The fire alarm has been going off for several minutes, but no one seems to notice, even though it's drowning out the person talking. A few people in the meeting start coughing due to the smoke.

Shockingly, they keep analyzing the numbers, oblivious to the fact that the building is about to go up in flames.

Sounds crazy, doesn't it? What company leaders—or what kind of people, for that matter—could possibly sit in a meeting with all that chaos and danger surrounding them? Yet, metaphorically, it happens every day in thousands of companies.

There are two different kinds of fires we're talking about. First, the everyday emergencies that crop up to steal your time—the day-to-day challenges you are unable to ignore.

Then there are the secondary fires: the things that, if left unattended, really could burn down your business. They are usually smoldering in the background and can ignite at any moment.

What you need are systems that allow you to focus on the real threats, instead of being in triage mode constantly.

That's why the first element in the Freedom Flywheel is "Fix the Fires." You can't build the business of your dreams based on chaos. Fires demand your attention, drain your energy, and keep you from focusing on the big picture.

> **IF YOU WANT FREEDOM AND CONTROL, YOU FIRST HAVE TO PUT OUT THE FIRES.**

Not every problem is a fire. Fires are the recurring, urgent issues, and sometimes embarrassing problems that refuse to die on their own. They tend to grow bigger and nastier the longer you ignore them. These fires don't just steal your time—they steal your momentum. And if you don't address them, they'll burn through your resources and your sanity.

Instead, you can free up time, energy, and bandwidth with some strategic fixes. It's not about perfection (for the perfectionists in the room)—it's about prioritizing what matters most and taking action.

Let's look at three ways to Fix the Fires: *practicing triage, paying to make the pain go away,* and *creating space for strategic thinking.*

PRACTICE TRIAGE

When I worked at the racetrack, chaos was my normal.

Here's a typical moment in my day. I'd have one horse who suddenly had a bellyache and was clearly uncomfortable. Another horse apparently had had a sore foot off and on over the past couple of days. And then there was always that one owner whose horse had been coughing occasionally for three weeks, but today was the day they finally decided it was a problem.

It was my job to assess the scene and answer these questions: Which issue is most urgent? Which one can wait? And which one might just be someone's overreaction?

Running a business is no different. Fires pop up everywhere. Your job is to figure out which deserve immediate action, and which can smolder a bit longer before they get doused.

Take a moment to ask yourself: What's stealing my time, energy, and focus? And more importantly, which of these things has the potential to do the most damage if left unattended?

Let's recap some of the usual suspects:

Risk: Unlike the obvious fires, unmanaged risk is like termites—you don't notice them eating away at the structure until the building begins to collapse. Mitigating risk isn't sexy, but addressing it is one of the cheapest and easiest ways to immediately increase the value and sustainability of your business.

Conduct a risk audit, including reviewing insurance policies and contracts, looking for compliance landmines, and creating contingency plans.

Cash Flow Crunches: Ever feel like your bills are due but your cash is playing a game of hide-and-seek? Maybe you've taken on a big client and had to front-load expenses—supplies, payroll, infrastructure—only to wait months before the money starts rolling in? Been there. It's not just frustrating; it's business threatening.

I learned this lesson the hard way:

> **PLANNING FOR CASH FLOW CRUNCHES DURING GROWTH SPURTS ISN'T JUST SMART—IT'S SURVIVAL.**

Bottlenecks: These traffic jams in your business processes leave clients waiting, blow past deadlines, and raise stress levels. Or employees are frustrated because they can't do their job well. We'll get more into this in Chapter Five.

Sometimes it's an issue outside your control, like a supply chain problem. But whether it's internal or external, bottlenecks need a solution—not an excuse.

People Problems: Toxic employees. Misaligned roles. Constant drama. It's exhausting at best, revenue draining at worst.

I recently worked with a client who had an employee who was less of a team player and more of a grenade with the pin pulled. He'd known for a while that this person had to go, but the thought of the confrontation (and paperwork) kept him stuck.

Problematic people drain your time, energy, and morale faster than you realize. Once my client finally took action, he couldn't believe the difference. The rest of the team stepped up, and the business began running more smoothly almost immediately.

You're not here to be a superhero. You can't fix every problem all at once. But you can focus on the fires that pose the greatest threat to your business's stability and momentum.

Key Takeaway: Don't try to fight every fire at once. Start with those that, if left burning, will cause the most damage. That's how you move from chaos to control—and from survival to strategy.

PAY TO MAKE THE PAIN GO AWAY

One of the hardest shifts we can make is moving from working *in* your business to working *on* it.

We all understand the concept—it's been around forever. But putting it into practice is a whole different thing than just knowing about it.

The basic concept is simple (yet oddly difficult): *You shouldn't be doing everything.* You need to identify the things only you can do, then delegate or outsource the rest to someone else.

I once had a client who would often work the phones at the front desk of her company. She didn't love doing it and wasn't even particularly good at it—it had simply become a habit. She could easily have had someone else doing it! She just never stopped to consider the alternatives.

We all fall into these ruts. We keep doing things out of habit or guilt, or even some weird sense of pride. Maybe we think it's easier and less time-consuming if we just do the thing ourselves.

I've been there. I remember being a new mom and working 24/7, doing "all the things." One of my business partners (a seasoned business veteran whose kids were grown) asked me, "Dawn, do you have a housekeeper? Who does your laundry?"

I blinked. "Um, me?"

"Why?" he said with a look on his face like I'd just confessed to a terrible sin. "Can't you afford to hire someone? That doesn't seem like a good use of your time."

I could definitely afford it, but it never occurred to me that I *should*. Let me tell you, the first time I walked into my freshly cleaned house to find order restored, the laundry done, and the bedsheets crisp and clean, it was life-changing!

That's just one small example. There are all sorts of "pains" you can pay someone to make go away.

Figure out what tasks you dread doing. Maybe it's accounting, marketing, or posting on social media. Maybe it's writing content. Maybe you need a social media assistant. Or like the former client I mentioned, maybe hire someone to answer the phones or do other administrative work. Perhaps it would be a huge relief to turn your financials and/or payroll over to a firm that specializes in it.

Think of it this way: Whatever you dislike doing (or is a waste of your precious time) is likely thrilling to someone else. Let them shine instead of making yourself do *everything*.

When you look at highly successful people, they are typically not doing things they find tedious or low-value. They have learned to outsource the pain points in their lives and businesses. They aren't successful because they work more hours than everyone else—their success is a result of them *spending their time where it counts.*

Sometimes business owners don't do this, though, because they're afraid of what others will think. I worked with a business owner who pushed back on this idea. She said, "I wouldn't want my employees to think that I feel those kinds of tasks are beneath me."

This is not about something being "beneath" you. It's about having the right mindset, knowing you only have so much time in your day. You need to use it on the most high-value tasks possible.

This isn't about ego, it's about math. If you can pay someone $20 an hour to handle tasks while you use that time to work on $200-an-hour problems, guess what? You just made $180 an hour. Where could you be making more money if your time was freed up from doing tasks you could easily delegate or outsource?

How to Track Your Time

Do you really know where your time is going? I recommend performing an activity audit.

> **EVERY DAY FOR TWO WEEKS, TRACK, IN THIRTY-MINUTE INCREMENTS, HOW YOU SPEND YOUR TIME.**

Write down what you're doing and for how long. The results will probably shock you.

Why? Because you'll likely find that you're spending vast amounts of time on things that you could easily—and cheaply—outsource to others.

We'll dive deeper into this process later in the book, but for now, let's keep it simple. Think of this as a quick start guide to reclaiming your brainpower:

Step 1: Identify one or two tasks to delegate immediately.

Maybe it's the bookkeeping that makes you want to cry, the endless social media posting, or the mountain of emails that never stop multiplying. Hand it off. Seriously, you have better things to do—like plotting world domination or binge-watching your favorite show guilt-free (depending on the day).

Step 2: Outsource or automate anything repetitive.

If you're still manually scheduling appointments and meetings, approving every little thing, or tracking receipts in a shoebox, it's time to find a better way. Technology and outsourcing can streamline these tasks and free up your time for more important priorities.

Step 3: Eliminate tasks that aren't serving you.

Some tasks don't need to be delegated or automated—they just need to disappear altogether. If you've been spending hours on things that don't actually move the needle or add value, it's time to let them go. Ask yourself: Does this task actually contribute to progress or profit (or is it legally required of my business)? If not, it's time to cross it off your list for good.

Key Takeaway: Some pains are worth paying to make go away because the return on investment (ROI) on your mental clarity is priceless.

CREATE SPACE FOR STRATEGIC THINKING

This is where the magic starts to happen. The whole goal of practicing triage and making the pain go away is to free you from low-value tasks so you have the time to think strategically.

Let me be blunt: You are never going to change anything if you're constantly stuck in the grind. You can't think creatively, dream big, or plot your next big move until you have the time and space to think.

One of the reasons good business coaching works so well is not because the coach has magic answers. It's because the process forces you to pause, asks the right questions, and gives you the space to consider them before answering them for yourself. Great coaches make sure you aren't just thinking about the tasks at hand. They're challenging you to look up and see the bigger picture.

> IT'S IMPOSSIBLE TO THINK OUTSIDE THE BOX WHEN YOU'RE STUCK INSIDE THE CHAOS. THAT'S WHY CARVING OUT TIME AND SPACE FOR REFLECTION MATTERS.

One of my mentors encouraged me to schedule thinking time every week. My response was, "Dude, I can't even get five minutes of peace without literally hiding out in the toilet."

He said, "You don't have time *not* to do this. Put it on your calendar."

I rolled my eyes. "I don't even use a calendar. I'm running around just putting out fires all the time."

He pushed back. "Okay. What time is it now? Four p.m. on Thursday. Every Thursday at four p.m., you're going to stop whatever you're doing. No exceptions. Put it aside so you can think. I don't want you solving problems. Instead, I want you to think about all the possibilities."

That conversation changed everything. What he was getting at was the importance of mindset. Scheduling dedicated strategic thinking time ultimately allowed me to make major moves like merging our business with other practices and eventually, launching my consulting business.

Until I made the space, I couldn't see the forest for the trees. But when I started to create space in my life for strategic thinking, everything started to change.

I used to think I was crushing it. I wasn't just a good doer—I was a *super doer*! If being busy was an Olympic sport, I'd have taken home gold, silver, and bronze. I worked hard, I worked fast, and I got a lot done.

But I wasn't actually getting anywhere. It was like running on a treadmill—lots of effort, zero forward momentum. It turns out that being busy doesn't guarantee progress, only exhaustion.

When I started creating space—giving myself one hour a week—to think strategically, everything shifted. I stopped just reacting to the day-to-day and started replacing chaos with clarity.

Key Takeaway: When you schedule strategic thinking time, you create a habit of looking at the view from thirty thousand feet and seeing all the possibilities. That's where real progress happens.

✿ ✿ ✿

Now that we've focused on fixing the fires in your business and you have some practical steps to move forward, let's turn our attention to something you can do when you free up time and energy for strategic thinking: reverse engineer your plan. Turn the page to find out how.

Reverse Engineer Your Plan

CHAPTER THREE

REVERSE ENGINEER YOUR PLAN

We kicked off the Freedom Flywheel with "Fix the Fires" for a reason. It's impossible to think about big-picture strategy when you're dodging metaphorical flames.

A crisis—whether it's financial, personnel-related, or operational—sucks up all the oxygen in the room. The goal of fixing those fires was to give you the space to step back and start seeing your business with clarity.

Now that you've got that space, it's time to start thinking about your overall vision.

This is the tricky part, though. The reason people struggle with vision is because it's hard to see past the reality of where you are right now.

That was always the challenge for me when I bought into my practice. It was a well-established business and they had been doing things the same way for a long time. It was hard to make meaningful changes because of the resistance I encountered.

I see this with business owners all the time. They'll say,

> "YOU DON'T UNDERSTAND—YOU CAN'T DO THAT IN MY BUSINESS. IT JUST WON'T WORK."

Translation: They're so used to the way things *are* that they can't imagine how they *could be*. All they can think about is how it's been done or how they're doing it now.

Most of the time, they're successful on some level. If it ain't broke, don't fix it, right? But remember, what got you *here* won't necessarily take you *there*.

That's why reverse engineering your plan is so critical. Lots of business owners are successful, but that doesn't necessarily mean it happened on purpose.

You don't want to leave *your* success to chance, so you've got to start with the end in mind, as Stephen Covey so brilliantly wrote about in *The 7 Habits of Highly Successful People*.

In this chapter we'll look at three keys to accomplishing that: *clarifying your vision and purpose, doing a brutal facts analysis,* and *mapping the journey.*

CLARIFY YOUR VISION AND PURPOSE

Terms like "vision" and "purpose" can feel vague. They sound like something you'd hear at a TED Talk right before the speaker launches into an inspiring story about climbing Mount Everest barefoot.

In theory at least, vision and purpose are the big ideas that guide our lives. However, most of us don't spend much time deliberately thinking about them.

We power through from year to year, decade to decade, wondering why we don't feel more successful or fulfilled.

But once we get clear on them, vision and purpose are like a GPS for our life and business.

What's Your Vision?

Think of vision as, well, an actual vision—something you see unfold like a movie on a giant screen. Imagine watching a preview of your future life where everything turns out just like you want it. You're the producer, director, and star of this film (and probably the lighting crew since entrepreneurs do it all), so dream big.

Most business owners hold back when it comes to vision. They'll say something vague like, "I want my company to grow." That's nice, but it's not a vision, it's a vague hope. Instead, paint a clear, vivid picture. "I want my company to double in revenue and to have locations in three countries over the next three years."

> **THE SPECIFICS MATTER.**
> **DON'T PLAY SMALL; CREATE A VISION**
> **BIG ENOUGH THAT IT FEELS**
> **A LITTLE UNCOMFORTABLE.**

Your vision is *yours*. Mentors, coaches, and authors (like me!) can help you brainstorm the possibilities, but no one can define your vision for you.

You have to *own* it.

What About Purpose?

Purpose is tied to your vision but it's not the same thing. If vision is about where you want to go, purpose is about why you're going there. It's what makes all the hard work, late nights, and tough decisions worth it.

Your purpose may be tied directly to your business. Maybe you want to provide jobs for your community, solve a problem no one else is addressing, or leave a legacy.

Or, your purpose might lie outside of your business. Maybe you want to spend more time volunteering, you dream of taking your grandkids on epic vacations (and actually having the energy to keep up with them), or you want to donate a big, show-stopping check to your favorite charity.

Whatever it is, that's your purpose.

And if your business isn't your life's passion, that's okay too. Plenty of people find themselves running businesses they didn't exactly choose. Maybe you inherited the role, fell into it by circumstance, or it just seemed like a good idea at the time.

Sometimes the purpose of your business is simply to provide the financial resources and freedom to allow you to pursue your passions. You don't have to intend to be the biggest or the best. Your purpose can be tailored so that it perfectly fits *you*.

Know Your Values

It's always best to make sure you know what your values are because they're the foundation for everything else.

When you think about what is most important to you in life right now, can you narrow it down to the top three things? When you go through this exercise, you may be surprised at how hard it is to get clarity on your values. I usually suggest you start by going through your values on a personal level.

Then ask yourself what you believe the core values of your business are. Are your personal core values in alignment with the core values of your business? They don't have to be the same, but they need to be able to coexist in harmony, or it won't feel good to you.

It's also important to remember to review your values periodically throughout your life, especially when you experience major changes. You may recall my story about how my priorities and what I valued changed after I became a parent, but I didn't pay attention and it got uncomfortable after a while.

If your business doesn't allow you to live in alignment with your personal values, you will always feel a disconnect.

GET MY "VET YOUR VISION" EXERCISE INCLUDED IN THIS BOOK'S BONUSES AT: PRODUCTIVEPRESSURE.COM/FLYWHEEL

The bottom line is that if you start thinking about your vision, and how everything ties into that, the path forward becomes much clearer.

Key Takeaway: Without a clear vision, you're just spinning your wheels. Without a purpose, you won't have the motivation to keep pushing when things get hard. And they will get hard!

DO A BRUTAL FACTS ANALYSIS

Once you have an idea of *what* you want and *why* you want it, you have to get super clear on where you are right now.

It might be painful. That's why I use the word "brutal." You're going to delve into not just your business finances—you're pulling back the curtain on everything. That includes your personal life and financial situation, even the parts you've been avoiding.

This is hard, especially as business owners, because we tend to wrap our identities up in what we do. If our business is doing well, we're a success. If it's struggling, we feel like we're failing.

This process is going to push some of those buttons. If you do this right, it may hurt, but it's going to be worth it.

You'll want to include all of your professional advisors—your accountant, financial planner, estate attorney—in this process. You'll need their help to gather all of the information you need for your brutal facts analysis. You're shooting for a completely transparent, no BS assessment of where you and your business stand at this moment in time.

You should include a business valuation, a review of your personal finances and your financial plan, consider your estate plan and associated tax strategies, as well as a review of any existing contracts and agreements.

This can be a little overwhelming, which is why I recommend professional help.

As a Business & Exit Strategist, I work with my clients' other trusted advisors to integrate all of that information into a cohesive plan. This is my superpower—I'm like a quarterback for the team. I don't block or tackle, I just support everyone else in their role, make sure the game plan is clear, and that we're all aiming for the same goal line.

Without that level of coordination, it can be difficult to see the full picture. Once you have this, it will be easier for you to understand what you need to accomplish to reach your goals.

If you don't have this information, you really don't know where you're starting from, so it's hard to plan the course for where you want to go. You need to know the gap between your vision and your current reality.

I worked with a business owner once who was convinced he needed $6 million to retire comfortably. He was grinding himself into the ground chasing this number, sacrificing time with his family and his health.

When we finally sat down with his financial planner for the brutal facts analysis, it turned out he needed only $5 million to live the life he wanted. That one-million-dollar difference changed everything. Knowing the real target allowed us to create a solid plan to get him there. Suddenly, his goals felt achievable. He could see the finish line.

The lesson? When you get clear on the gap—whether it's a wealth gap, a value gap, or just the gap between your expectations and reality—everything else becomes logistics. You can stop guessing and start planning.

Here's what I recommend you do next:

1. *Gather Your Team:* You're going to need your accountant, financial planner, and lawyer. If you don't have these people, get them. You wouldn't try to rebuild an engine without a mechanic, and you shouldn't try to untangle your financial situation without experts.

2. ***Get Your Business Valuation:*** This is where you find out what your business is *actually* worth—not what you think it's worth after scrolling through social media and seeing someone claim they sold a company for 10x revenue. This can be sobering, but it's a critical step.

3. ***Do a Gap Analysis:*** This includes the following:

   - *Wealth Gap:* What do you have now, and what do you need to live the life you want?

   - *Value Gap:* How much is your business worth today, and how much does it need to be worth to meet your financial goals and close your wealth gap?

   - *Purpose Gap:* Is your business aligned with your personal values and purpose, or is it just a means to an end? Having clarity on this may determine what you want your role in the business to be going forward—if you even want to continue to work *in* the business.

Key Takeaway: Understanding where you are today is the foundation for getting where you want to go.

MAP THE JOURNEY

Once you've clarified your vision and purpose (where you're going and why) and have done a brutal facts analysis (where you are), the next logical step is *how* to get from here to there. It's time to map the journey.

This is where you come up with a concrete plan to get the freedom and financial security you want, both now and later.

As a business owner, it's easy to fall into the "someday" trap—feeling like you have to grind away for years or decades, toughing it out and sucking it up until you can *finally* retire and enjoy your life at some undetermined point in the future.

But what if you could enjoy life both in the future *and* right now? What if you could have freedom *now* instead of deferring it for thirty years?

We'll get into the specifics of how to do this in later chapters. But for now, let's work on reverse engineering your plan from there to here.

Assuming you didn't make any adjustments to your vision or purpose after completing your brutal facts analysis, the next step is just about connecting the dots.

Here's where the reverse engineering comes in. You need to start with where you want to end up and plot the journey back to where you are today.

For example, five years from now the owner of a $4 million business wants to sell it for $6 million. Cool. So, what does it need to be worth three years from now? One year from now? What needs to happen in each of those times frames to support that growth?

Once you know what needs to happen in the next year, break it down further into ninety-day (quarterly) sprints. During each sprint, you'll focus on certain goals that will drive the results you want and need. From there you'll create action plans and assign ownership and accountability to team members.

The more granular you get, the more likely you are to be successful. At the end of the day, most strategic plans fail because while they might look cool, they lack implementation and a rhythm for consistent accountability.

I never said this way easy! It's anything but. However, just like you've probably noticed, the things in life—and business—that are worth the most, are often the hardest. And they're absolutely worth it.

Key Takeaway: Once you're clear on your vision and why, the rest is just logistics. Your plan for the journey will guide every decision and action.

✿ ✿ ✿

In the next chapter, we'll dive into one of my favorite keys of the Freedom Flywheel— embracing metrics that matter.

It's easy to get distracted by all the data and numbers available to us in our business. But now that you're armed with a way to fix the fires and reverse engineer your plan, it's time to get a bit more granular and take a look at your most important metrics. That's the topic of Chapter Four.

Embrace
Metrics
That Matter

EMBRACE METRICS THAT MATTER

Welcome to the third element of the Freedom Flywheel: metrics. Wait, don't roll your eyes just yet.

I know metrics don't sound exciting. If this were a movie, it would be the part where someone pulls out a spreadsheet and half the audience walks out.

Stick with me, though. This is one of the most important chapters in this entire book. Why? In order to successfully follow your reverse engineered plan, you need to measure your progress regularly along the way. And without mastering this, you won't reach your goals—and you wouldn't even know if you did!

This doesn't mean just tracking your numbers, it means identifying and monitoring the *right* metrics for your business.

When you focus on the *right* numbers instead of getting distracted by the *wrong* numbers, they can tell you the real story of your business. They can show you where to focus your energy so you can have more freedom, more profitability … and, most importantly, more *fun*!

So, let's dive into three key concepts that will make this both actionable and (dare I say it again) fun: *ignoring vanity metrics, focusing on the right metrics*, and *then taking appropriate action*.

IGNORE VANITY METRICS

Let's start with a confession: I've fallen for vanity metrics before. Who hasn't at some point?

These are metrics designed to make you look and feel good, rather than actually being helpful or relevant. Think of vanity metrics like the social media highlights reel of your business: They look impressive at first glance, but they don't tell the whole story.

A lot of people love to focus on revenue—specifically, top-line revenue. That money your business is bringing in every month, every quarter, every year, whatever.

People love bragging about revenue. "We're an eight-figure business!" But revenue is just the money coming in; it doesn't necessarily mean you're keeping any of it. Even if your business is pulling in $10 million, if your expenses are $9,500,000 that's not a great ROI.

If you have a highly efficient business that's lean but you're only making high six figures, your business might actually be worth more than a seven-figure business that's burning through cash and has crazy high expenses.

Another vanity metric can be profit. Now, of course, profit matters—it's a key indicator of success. But it doesn't necessarily mean that your business is *valuable*. And it definitely doesn't guarantee your cash flow is good.

On paper, your profit might look solid—your income is greater than your expenses. But there are all sorts of dynamics that can make things tricky.

For example, if your business relies heavily on accounts receivable, it might look like you have "earned" a lot of money. But if people haven't paid you, that cash isn't in your pocket.

You'll be paying taxes on that money, even if you haven't actually received it—and that's the kind of cash flow crunch that can sink a business. Even one that looks profitable on paper. This is why it's important to look at metrics that actually matter to you and your business.

It's easy to get too focused on the wrong financial metrics, but it's also easy to focus on other metrics that don't necessarily correlate with the value of your business.

Another metric a lot of business owners want to show off is their "team." Some owners love the appearance of success and the sense of energy and confidence that comes from hiring people.

However, the number of people on your payroll has no direct connection to the value of your business. In fact, it often means more expenses and more headaches, and usually there is a gap between bringing them on board and the income that will (hopefully and eventually) result from their contributions.

Vanity metrics aren't just harmless distractions. They can actively lead you astray. Focusing on the wrong numbers can lead to wasting time, energy, and resources on things that don't matter. They can also give you a false sense of security by making you feel like all is well … when it's not.

Sounds pretty simple, right? But you'd be surprised how many owners fall into this trap.

Key Takeaway: The wrong metrics waste your time and energy. Focus on the numbers that drive value, not just revenue and profits.

FOCUS ON THE RIGHT METRICS

Not all metrics are created equal. Some are necessary for making smart decisions, while others just clutter your dashboard (more on that below). The key is to focus on the right numbers.

If vanity metrics aren't the answer, what should you be focusing on? The metrics that truly matter depend on your specific business, but there are a few things to consider:

Leading vs. Trailing Metrics: Trailing metrics, like revenue and profit, tell you what's already happened. Leading metrics such as customer inquiries, website traffic, or sales pipeline activity give you insight into what's coming next. A balanced focus on both leading and trailing metrics ensures you're proactive rather than reactive.

OKRs and KPIs: Objectives and Key Results (OKRs) and Key Performance Indicators (KPIs) are essential tools for aligning your team around measurable goals. While KPIs track *ongoing performance* in specific areas, OKRs help you set ambitious, *time-bound objectives*. For example, a KPI might track monthly sales growth, while an OKR might set a goal to increase sales by 25 percent in the next quarter.

Some universal metrics to consider tracking:

Revenue Growth Rate: Is your business growing or dying? We're going to talk more about growth in Chapter Six, but monitoring this can help you assess the impact of your sales strategies, customer demand, and market conditions. Sustainable growth is also a key factor in maximizing value.

EBITDA (Earnings Before Interest, Taxes, Depreciation, and Amortization): It's the go-to profitability metric for buyers because it focuses only on what the business actually earns from operations. It's a great snapshot of whether your business is profitable, scalable, and valuable.

Operating Cash Flow: If revenue is the heart of your business, cash flow is the blood. It's what keeps the lights on and the doors open. Are you collecting payments on time? Are you holding too much inventory? Cash flow metrics tell you how well your business is running day-to-day.

Customer Lifetime Value (LTV): How much revenue does the average customer bring in over the course of their relationship with you? This number helps you understand the long-term value of your customer base and informs decisions about marketing and retention.

Customer Acquisition Cost (CAC): How much are you spending to acquire a new customer? Compare this with your LTV to ensure you're not spending more to acquire customers than they're worth.

Profit Margins: Your profit margin tells you how efficiently your business turns revenue into profit. High revenue with low margins is a warning sign.

Employee Efficiency: Revenue or profit per employee can be a great way to measure whether your team is operating effectively. Are you getting the most out of your payroll investment?

How can you tell if your numbers are "good?" Start by taking a look at the benchmarks in your industry. Use sources like trade associations, financial and market research platforms, benchmarking tools and software, or an industry-savvy CPA. While they may not be exactly comparable to your business, they can usually give you a good indication of where you're doing well and where there's room for improvement.

Key Takeaway: Metrics should guide decisions, not overwhelm you. Track a few key numbers that align with your goals.

USE METRICS TO DRIVE ACTION

Now that you've determined the metrics you want to track and you have benchmarks to guide your analysis, it's time to break down your long-term goals into short-term actions. If your goal is to increase profit margins by 5 percent this year, what needs to happen this quarter? This month? This week? Next, add your targets to your reverse engineered plan from Chapter Three.

Then you'll want to create a dashboard (this could be as simple as a whiteboard or spreadsheet, or as sophisticated as a custom software application, depending on your needs). The dashboard allows you to have a current and clear view of the numbers that matter to you and your team.

Here's where the magic happens (or doesn't!).

> **METRICS ARE ONLY VALUABLE IF YOU USE THEM TO MAKE DECISIONS AND TAKE ACTION.**
> **WITHOUT ACTION, METRICS ARE JUST NUMBERS ON A PAGE.**

I once worked with a client who was obsessed with tracking their marketing metrics. They had spreadsheets full of data on click-through rates, social media engagement, and website traffic.

But when I asked how they were using that data, they admitted they weren't doing much with it. They were so busy analyzing that they hadn't made any changes to improve their marketing strategy.

This is what's known as analysis paralysis. It's easy to get so caught up in the data that you forget to use it to drive action.

Start by asking yourself questions like:

Where are the biggest leaks in my business? Metrics like cash flow and profit margins can help you identify inefficiencies or unnecessary expenses.

What's driving growth? Look at your most profitable products, services, or customer segments and focus your energy there.

What's holding me back? Metrics can highlight bottlenecks, whether it's a slow production process, low employee productivity, or high customer churn.

It's not just about you as the business owner understanding the metrics either—it's about getting that information out to your team. They need to be able to connect the vision with how they spend their time each day.

Delegate responsibility to your team for tracking and improving key metrics. Empower them to take ownership and be part of the solution. When everyone understands how their role impacts the bigger picture, it creates alignment and momentum. And it's your job as the leader to make that clear connection.

Key Takeaway: Metrics are only useful if they lead to action. Don't just track them—use them to transform.

✿ ✿ ✿

Remember, metrics are like the GPS of your business. They keep you on track and show you what steps to take next.

But it's essential to track *what matters*.

Don't get caught up in vanity metrics. Focus on the right numbers, take action on what they're communicating to you, and you'll be set up to become more independent from your business. That's the topic of Chapter Five.

Establish
Owner
Independence

ESTABLISH OWNER INDEPENDENCE

Here is one of the great ironies of entrepreneurship: Many people decide to step away from a regular job in order to have the "freedom" of being a business owner. But in the end, they find that they're working much longer hours with more responsibility, more stress, and more risk.

You're supposed to be the one who's an owner, right? But many people who become entrepreneurs discover that the business owns *them*.

I want to help you establish independence from your business. If your business revolves around you, it's not scalable, sustainable, or ultimately as valuable as it could be.

It's a hard pill to swallow, I know. You've poured your blood, sweat, and tears into it. It's part of you. Many owners think of their business as their "baby."

> **BUT YOUR BUSINESS IS NOT YOUR BABY. AND IF YOUR BUSINESS CAN'T RUN WITHOUT YOU, THEN IT'S NOT A BUSINESS, IT'S JUST A JOB— THE KIND OF JOB WHERE YOU'RE THE FIRST ONE IN, THE LAST ONE TO LEAVE, AND THE ONE WHO GETS THE CALL WHEN ANYTHING GOES WRONG.**

While you may have lots of emotions and feelings tied to it, but I want to remind you that you are reading this book because you believe your business should be a financial asset that can be sold. Which also means it can increase in value and give you an impactful return.

In this chapter, we'll take a look at three interrelated issues to help you create a self-managing business: *dealing with the hard truth that you might be the bottleneck, understanding the roles of delegation, automation, and systems,* and *creating more leadership depth.*

ARE YOU THE BOTTLENECK?

"Bottleneck owners" believe they have to be the person making all the decisions and have their finger on the pulse of every part of their business.

If you're the bottleneck in your business, it doesn't mean you're a bad person or necessarily a bad leader. You're probably incredibly hard-working, dedicated, and passionate about your business. You've probably built it from the ground up and feel incredibly connected to every part of it. You care about it more than anyone else. And you may be stuck in the belief that if you don't do it yourself, it won't get done right.

Two types of owners fall into this category. One type is the bottleneck who hasn't realized it … yet. The second type knows they're the bottleneck, but they can't see any other way of doing things.

If neither of these describe you, congrats! You've done a great job pulling out of tasks that would eat up your time and energy—tasks that you've handed off to others so you can focus on more important things.

But maybe, like many people I work with, you feel you're somewhere in the middle. You don't think of yourself as a micromanager, but you know there are definitely some things you could delegate to others.

I know it's hard when you're caught up in the day-to-day rush of running your business. It's a challenge to find time to think about what you should get off your plate, and then execute a plan to make it happen.

Maybe you don't have the right people in the right roles, you don't know who to choose, or you don't think you can afford it. Maybe you've never learned how to delegate effectively.

For now, the most important thing is realizing that you need to give more thought to sharing the load so your business can start running without you. As they say, the first step to overcoming a problem is admitting you have one.

Key Takeaway: Admitting you're the center of everything is hard, but it's the first step toward creating freedom—for you and your business.

ELIMINATE, DELEGATE, AUTOMATE

Let me share a simple, game-changing framework for business owner independence: Eliminate, Delegate, Automate. These three practices form a cycle of productivity and freedom.

Once you put them into motion, they'll help you reclaim your time, refocus your energy, and run your business instead of letting it run you.

Step 1: Eliminate

Let's start with the easiest question: What doesn't need to exist in your workday at all?

This is where the activity audit is really important. If you already did it in Chapter Two, great! If not, here's a quick recap: Track everything you do for a week in thirty-minute increments.

No judgment, no editing—just log it all. Whether you're scrolling through your inbox, negotiating with vendors, or googling how to reset the Wi-Fi router for the third time this week, write it down.

Then take a hard look at the list and ask yourself: What's a total waste of time? What's not moving the needle in my business?

If you're being honest, you'll probably have to admit that there's some fluff on that list. Meetings that could've been emails. Tasks you're doing out of habit. Things you keep doing simply because you haven't really thought about why you need to be doing them at all.

The quickest win here is to eliminate the activities that aren't adding value. If you want to take it a step further, you can create a "not-to-do" list to remind you of the things you're committed to *not* doing anymore!

Step 2: Delegate

We talked about this in Chapter Two: Fix the Fires. After you've eliminated the fluff, identify what's left that does need to get done—but doesn't need to be done by you.

Let's face it: As business owners, we're pros at holding on to things we shouldn't. We say things like:

- "It's faster if I just do it myself."

- "No one else can do it as well as I can."
- "But what if they screw it up?"

Maybe we calculate how much time it will take us to train someone in the task and don't recognize those extra minutes will save hours in the months that follow. Someone else can do it, and the world won't end if they do it a little differently than you would. Delegation isn't about giving up control—it's about focusing on the work only you can do and letting your team (or external resources) handle the rest.

Not only will you free up time for yourself to work on higher-value projects, but you'll also allow others to learn new skills and take on more responsibility.

You can begin training your delegation muscles by starting with low-risk tasks. Try handing off repetitive admin work to an assistant, having someone else manage your email or customer inquiries, or delegating social media scheduling to a team member. Eventually, you will work up to outsourcing bigger projects that your team can't handle.

The goal isn't to offload your entire workload overnight—it's to chip away at the unnecessary and reclaim your bandwidth bit by bit.

> **DELEGATION DONE WELL
> IS A GIFT TO BOTH YOU AND
> THE PERSON YOU SHARE THE
> RESPONSIBILITY WITH.**

Step 3: Automate

Finally, automation. If a task can't be eliminated or delegated, ask yourself: Can it be automated?

Automation is your secret weapon for streamlining the repetitive tasks that eat away at your time. For example:

- **Micromanaging inventory and supply chain issues:** Use AI-driven systems to forecast demand and plan inventory levels. Automate vendor communication with software systems and let your well-trained staff resolve any problems.

- **Following up on sales leads:** Use your customer relationship management (CRM) system to automate lead nurturing and let your sales team focus on closing. That way *you* can focus on scaling!

- **Approving every IT purchase:** Use a procurement tool to set preapproved vendor lists and budget caps. Your time is better spent leveraging the tech ... to automate more tasks.

Start small. You don't need to go full tech-wizard with advanced software right away. Even basic automation—like automated scheduling or email automations—can save you hours every month. The key is to focus on automating tasks that drain your time or energy unnecessarily.

When you combine elimination, delegation, and automation, you create a system that frees you to focus on what truly matters—whether that's strategic planning, growing your business, or finally enjoying a guilt-free weekend.

This isn't just theory. I've seen it work for countless business owners. A couple of quick examples:

A client of mine was spending twelve hours a week manually invoicing clients. After delegating part of it to an assistant and automating the rest, they reclaimed that time to focus on building relationships with key clients and following up on new leads.

Within a few months, they saw a noticeable improvement in client retention and a steady increase in sales—proof that freeing up your time can drive meaningful growth where it matters most.

Another client was bogged down handling their own customer onboarding. By creating a streamlined process, delegating support to their team, and automating reminders, they cut onboarding time in half and improved customer satisfaction.

Every hour you free up is an hour you can reinvest in high-value work—or you can use it to just breathe a little easier.

Key Takeaway: Freedom doesn't come from doing everything—it comes from empowering others and creating systems that run themselves.

LEADERSHIP DEPTH

Understanding that you may be a bottleneck, then taking actions like eliminating, delegating, or automating tasks you shouldn't be doing are important steps toward going deeper as a leader.

But having a sustainable business requires more than just a great leader. It requires a culture of leadership throughout the organization. Take it from a recovering superhero—if you are the most important person in your business, not only is it not sustainable, but you also might be doing it wrong!

In an earlier chapter, I mentioned that I did a great job of whipping our business into shape. It was a lean, mean, well-oiled machine, with one exception. We had no leadership depth.

My partner and I were the rainmakers in our business, and proud of it! I was so integral to the day-to-day success of our business that I worked six to seven days a week. I was on call 24/7 until the day I gave birth to my first child.

Believe it or not, I went to work in labor because there was no one to cover for me that day. And when I came back three weeks later with a newborn and nanny in tow, I was a legend! And then I did it again with my second kid. (Of course, it was less impressive the second time around because I'd already shown it could be done.)

My "heroic" behavior meant that no matter how well the business ran when I was there, it fell apart when I wasn't. We had designed it that way. Looking back, I understand that it was a critical mistake.

As a business leader and owner, the goal is to be working *on* your business, doing high-level strategic thinking, more than working *in* your business.

When you're starting out, it's unavoidable to be doing all the things, but it's important *not* to get stuck in that role! Otherwise, you've bought yourself a job, not a business. That's exactly what I had done.

Have you ever been afraid to go on vacation because you were worried things might fall apart in your absence? Maybe you thought, *What if the team makes the wrong decisions? What if customers leave? What if there's some other crisis I haven't anticipated?*

Or maybe you've experienced this: Every time you do go on vacation you're exhausted by the preparation to leave. Then you try to spend a few days winding down while constantly checking your phone for messages and emails. Before your vacation is over, you're already dreading what will be waiting for you when you get back.

> **LEADERSHIP DEPTH IS ALL ABOUT BUILDING A SELF-MANAGING BUSINESS. ONE THAT DOESN'T NEED YOU TO FUNCTION.**

This means your team can make decisions, solve problems, and keep things running—even when you're not around.

It's about creating an environment where your people have autonomy over their roles, continuously improve their skills, and understand their purpose within the larger company vision.

Ultimately, your goal is to build a team that can operate and thrive without you. Because if your business grinds to a halt the moment you step away (or you're afraid it will), you don't have freedom.

You want to be replaceable.

> **THE MORE REPLACEABLE YOU ARE, THE STRONGER YOUR BUSINESS BECOMES.**

Here are some ways to create leadership depth:

Delegate Authority, Not Just Tasks: Don't keep all the decision-making power for yourself. Give your team the authority to make meaningful decisions and trust them to handle it.

Develop Future Leaders: Create a leadership succession plan. Invest in training, mentorship, and growth opportunities for your team. The more skilled and confident they are, the more they'll step up.

Document Processes: Create systems and standard operating procedures (SOPs) so that anyone can step into a role and know what to do. Think of it as "business insurance."

Test Your Team's Independence: Step away for a week. Then two. See how the business performs without you. Identify gaps and adjust. The goal is to make your absence a nonevent.

When you build leadership depth, a few amazing things happen:

First, your operations improve because everything doesn't depend on you.

Second, your risk decreases, which boosts the value of your business.

And third, you get to experience actual freedom—the kind where you can take a vacation without checking your email every hour.

An added bonus to all of this is as your team takes more ownership of your business, morale improves and profits grow.

Becoming more independent from your business gives you the ability to focus on what really matters—whether that's scaling to new heights or enjoying life outside of work.

And here's the reality check: 80 percent of businesses available for sale fail to sell. Buyers don't want to buy your job—they want to invest in a *self-sustaining*, scalable company that runs independently.

Key Takeaway: Building leadership depth is about more than just protecting your business—it's about creating a *self-managing business* that gives you freedom now and more value when you're ready to sell.

✿ ✿ ✿

This chapter might be the hardest one in the book to implement. Why? Because looking at your leadership requires a huge amount of honesty and self-reflection.

It's hard to admit that we might be holding our business back even though we want the best for it. Just like a parent who is facing an empty nest when their kids go off to college, every business owner has to realize that their "baby" needs to be separated from them at some point. It's a natural part of growth.

And the best part? When you intentionally become more independent from your business, not only can the business grow—you'll grow, too. It's an essential part of building more freedom into your life.

That independence also gives you the time, space, and energy to focus on driving greater growth for your business and yourself. We'll look at that next, in Chapter Six.

Drive Growth and Scalability

DRIVE GROWTH AND SCALABILITY

There's a saying in business that if you're not growing, you're dying. If you aren't focused on growth, then most likely you're going to shrink. It's almost impossible to maintain the status quo. It's like trying to balance on a bicycle without pedaling—eventually, you're going to tip over.

Why? Because things change. It becomes more expensive to deliver your product or your service. You lose clients. Your industry evolves. You go through a personal crisis of some kind.

That said, you don't just want to grow for the sake of getting bigger. Growth is accompanied by cost and risk, depending on how you're trying to grow.

THAT'S WHY GROWTH SHOULD BE STRATEGIC, SUSTAINABLE, AND ALIGNED WITH YOUR VISION.

There are different types of growth. You can grow internally by taking on more customers, adding products or services to your core offerings, or exploring new verticals. External growth can come from acquiring other businesses like yours (potentially offering economies of scale) or those that give you a strategic advantage.

The possibilities are endless. But the bottom line is that sustainable growth is about doing the right things—not just doing more things. Growth should amplify your success, not your stress.

This chapter explores how to *build for scalability, prioritize what matters most,* and *use productive pressure to grow or scale without breaking.*

BUILD FOR SCALABILITY

One of the keys to scalability is having systems and processes in place. Once you have those, as well as clearly documented SOPs, you can easily add more to the system without needing a lot more people or financial input. It's much more efficient.

Scaling is different from growth. Growth is increasing output by adding resources proportionately. But with scaling, you're aiming for significantly increased output with your existing resources (or minimal additional resources).

Systems and processes are what allow you to create scale.

Spending time creating strong and efficient systems and processes makes your company more efficient, more sustainable, and more valuable. You should have systems and processes in place across all departments in your company.

Your systems, processes, and automations should all be thoroughly documented, usually through detailed written instructions and videos. They should be "live," readily accessible, and updated regularly by whoever uses them.

This is not just because it's more convenient for the people in the role now—SOPs are also incredibly valuable when it comes time to sell your company.

Write the SOPs in such a way that someone with very little training could perform the process or understand the system.

SOPs make it much easier to "plug and play" new employees into an existing system. This decreases training and onboarding costs and makes the business more sustainable.

If you don't leverage well-documented systems and processes in your business, not only is it difficult to grow, you'll end up with unnecessary bottlenecks.

I once had a client who kept pushing back against automating some of the bookkeeping practices in her business. She felt that if she wasn't writing the checks and delivering the receipts to the bookkeeper, she wouldn't be able to stay on top of the finances.

It was taking a lot of the owner's time and becoming a major drain on the business, which had grown to the point where it was impacting its ability to grow.

The owner's mindset was that the accountant wasn't able to do their job well, let alone do good tax accounting. The accountant didn't have timely financials since the owner would take all the receipts at the end of the month, write all her paper checks, and then report them when she received the bank statements.

As a result, they were always a couple of months behind in their bookkeeping. Not only was the owner spending too much time in this area, there was also a huge opportunity cost because of the constant bookkeeping delay. They couldn't make informed strategic decisions because their information was always a couple of months old.

All this requires a big mindset shift. You may have done things the same way for a long time. But spending a little time creating better systems and improving your mindset pays huge dividends later on. These are two areas I spend a lot of time on with my clients because they have an impact on every phase of the flywheel.

Key Takeaway: Scalability is about creating systems and capacity that can amplify your output without significantly increasing your costs or straining your resources.

FOCUS ON WHAT MATTERS MOST

The secret to *growing* the right way isn't about doing more—it's about doing the right things, at the right time, in the right ways.

Growth is not a badge of honor if it leaves you exhausted, overextended, and watching your business teeter on the edge of chaos. That's why the 80/20 Rule is your best friend. It says that 80 percent of your results come from 20 percent of your efforts, so your job is to identify which 20 percent is moving the needle and then laser-focus on it. This isn't about working harder—it's about working smarter.

Let's take a quick look at a few of the high-impact areas where growth can happen when you focus on what truly matters:

High-Value Customers: Think about your best customers—those who are profitable, easy to work with, and aligned with your business values.

They're probably the 20 percent that drives 80 percent of your revenue. What makes them such a great fit? How can you attract more clients like them?

Stop spreading your marketing efforts thin. Double down on finding and serving more of those customers. Build loyalty programs, ask for referrals, and create specialized offerings that cater to their specific needs.

Retention Over Acquisition: Customer acquisition is exciting, but let's face it—it's also expensive. Studies show it costs five times more to gain a new customer than it does to keep an existing one. If you've already won a customer's trust, why not nurture that relationship? Focus on providing exceptional service, upselling complementary products or services, and creating experiences that keep customers coming back, especially the top 20 percent we identified above.

A subscription or recurring revenue model could be a great way to retain customers. When done right, these models provide consistent cash flow and make your business more attractive to buyers.

Expanding Markets: Growth doesn't always mean doing something brand new. Apply the 80/20 Rule to your growth strategy too. Sometimes, it's about taking what's already working and expanding it into a new market. Maybe that's a geographic market, an industry niche, or even a demographic you haven't targeted before.

For example, let's say you run a successful pet care business in one city. Expanding into neighboring cities might be the easiest, fastest way to grow without reinventing the wheel.

Acquisitions: This is one of the most powerful—but often overlooked—ways to grow. Buying another business can give you a fast track to scaling. Why? Because that acquired business can give you instant access to new markets, amazing cross-selling opportunities, new talent and IP, and so much more. It can be especially powerful if your acquisition aligns with the 20 percent of your efforts that drive your biggest wins.

Let's say you own a landscaping company in the suburbs. You find a smaller, struggling company in the same space that operates in a nearby urban market. By acquiring them, you gain access to their customer list, hire their skilled employees, and expand into a new geographic area—without starting from scratch.

Keep in mind that not all growth is good growth. It's easy to fall into the trap of saying yes to every opportunity that comes your way, thinking that more is always better.

But the truth is, saying yes to everything can leave you overstretched and overwhelmed.

The key is to focus on aligned growth—opportunities that match your vision, play to your strengths, and make the most of your resources.

Key Takeaway: Growth isn't about doing more—it's about doing what matters most. Whether you're expanding markets, focusing on customer retention, or exploring acquisitions, the goal is to amplify your success without multiplying your stress.

USE PRODUCTIVE PRESSURE

Once your systems are humming along and your growth strategy is determined, it's time to talk about productive pressure.

This isn't about pushing harder—it's about pushing smarter. It's about applying just enough pressure to create focus, urgency, and results—without tipping over into stress and chaos. Think of it as the accelerator on your growth/scalability engine.

Here are a few ways to leverage productive pressure effectively:

Set Boundaries to Focus Efforts: Growth doesn't happen by accident—it happens when you intentionally focus your energy on what matters most. That means saying no to distractions (even the shiny ones) and setting boundaries around your time, priorities, and resources.

Leverage Constraints to Innovate: Constraints aren't roadblocks—they're tools that force you to clarify what's truly important. Believe it or not, having too much time, money, or freedom can actually hurt your growth. Why? Because constraints are where creativity thrives. When resources are limited, you're forced to think strategically, streamline processes, and innovate in ways you wouldn't otherwise. Constraints, when applied thoughtfully, unlock opportunity.

Create Accountability Loops: We all know that when you set goals and review them, you're more likely to achieve them. The key is consistent check-ins, not micromanagement. Whether it's a team meeting, your progress dashboard, or a quick message, accountability keeps everyone focused and aligned.

Push—but Don't Break: Productive pressure creates balance. You want to push just enough to stretch your team's capabilities and drive results, but not so much that your systems or people start to crack. If you find deadlines slipping, quality dropping, or morale tanking, it's time to recalibrate.

Again, the pressure isn't mean to overwhelm you. Instead, it should drive innovation and help both you and your team to be more efficient and effective.

Key Takeaway: The key to growth and scalability isn't sprinting to the finish line—you want to run a smart, sustainable race. With systems in place and the right amount of productive pressure, you can grow/scale your business without breaking what you've built.

✿ ✿ ✿

The bottom line here is that growth doesn't have to mean chaos. By focusing on building for scalability, pursuing the right opportunities, and applying productive pressure, you *can* hit your goals faster without breaking what you've built.

Everything we have talked about in previous chapters plays into this. If you haven't fixed the fires, reverse engineered your plan, embraced metrics that matter, and made time to work *on* your business instead of *in* your business, it's going to be pretty hard to drive growth.

But don't get discouraged! This is a process. And it takes time. Most business owners I know—including me!—are not the most patient people on planet Earth.

Somehow, we have to maintain a balance between keeping our foot on the gas and realizing that Rome wasn't built in a day. Neither will the ideal version of your business.

The great news is that when you have given attention to these first five keys of the Freedom Flywheel, you'll be set up in an amazing way to tackle the topic of Chapter Seven: Optimize Profitability.

Optimize
Profitability

OPTIMIZE PROFITABILITY

Although profitability is the sixth item in the Freedom Flywheel, it's probably the real reason why you're here.

After all, money is the lifeblood of your business. Without profit, you have no freedom—you're stuck in survival mode. You can't pay to hire people, make the pain go away, or even keep the lights on.

If you have profit—and, of course, cash flow—you have leverage. Leverage to take risks. Leverage to grow. Even leverage to step back and enjoy the business you've worked so hard to grow. You can be strategic.

Increased profitability doesn't just mean earning more—it means keeping more of what you already make, using your resources more wisely, and putting your money to work for you.

The easiest place to start is with low-hanging fruit and quick wins.

PROFIT BUCKETS

If your business is a leaky bucket, you want to fix all the leaks. So, before you explore exciting and creative ways to be more profitable, you need to take care of the basics. Any unnecessary costs, inefficiencies, and lost opportunities are draining your hard-earned cash.

There are many ways to do this, but here are a few simple ideas to get you started:

- *Audit Your Subscriptions and Software Licenses:* Organizations often end up with overlapping or underutilized software licenses. Do you really need seven design tools? Cancel any you don't need.

- *Review Vendor Contracts:* Negotiate better terms or find new vendors. I once saved a client $20,000 a year by switching one of their suppliers.

- *Streamline Operations:* If your team is spending hours manually entering data, invest in software to automate it. Yes, it costs up front, but inefficiency is even more expensive.

- ***Pay Attention to Energy and Overhead:*** Switch to LED lights. Maintain your HVAC. Adjust your thermostat when necessary. Stop printing everything in color. Those small tweaks add up, especially in larger companies.

Once you've plugged the leaks in your bucket, you'll want to turn your attention to the fun stuff ahead in this chapter: *uncovering hidden profit opportunities, turning cash flow into a powerful tool for growth and flexibility,* and *maximizing margins.*

UNCOVER HIDDEN PROFITS

When we think about profitability, we naturally want to look at expenses we can cut. That's typically the first impulse of a business owner who is looking to be more profitable.

I want you to not only plug the leaks but also find sources of revenue you may not have considered before. I call these "revenue gaps." These might be underperforming products or services you either need to improve or discontinue.

We like to hang on to revenue streams because it feels like any income is good income. But just like customers who aren't serving your business well, you can have income streams that aren't serving you well either.

We've all had customers who have cost us too much time and money. The same can be true for some verticals. Maybe you have a whole product line that's underperforming. You tried everything to fix it, but nothing is working.

Painful as it is to admit it, it's probably time to let it go.

Starbucks recently announced that they are trimming back their overcomplicated menu. They were used to adding specialty and seasonal items to the menu without taking anything away. The result was a bloated menu that was increasingly hard to navigate. For every new item added, one more complexity for workers was added, too. They chose to streamline and have discontinued products that don't sell well or have profit margins that are too low.

> **SOMETIMES THE EASIEST WAY TO MAKE MONEY IS TO TAKE SOME THINGS AWAY.**

When you combine that with maximizing your existing revenue, it's a powerful strategy to be more profitable.

Consider doing things like upselling, cross-selling, increasing customer retention, and looking at your pricing strategies. Even small changes in your pricing strategies can make a big difference in your profitability.

Key Takeaway: Take a look at all your current offerings and reduce or get rid of the things that aren't profitable.

TURN CASH FLOW INTO A POWER TOOL

We all know that cash is king!

In many ways, cash flow matters more than revenue. You could be making millions in sales but still be broke if your cash flow is a mess.

This can be a real challenge for seasonal businesses. Their revenue is often concentrated at certain times of the year, but their fixed costs are often year-round. They will have cash surpluses during busy seasons and cash shortages during off-peak times.

This requires excellent cash flow management to avoid straining the company's ability to cover operating costs, maintain inventory, or invest in growth.

Growth is great. Increasing revenue is great. But if you don't have the cash flow to support it, you can get into real trouble. That's why you need to build reserves, so you have a buffer for those lean or uncertain times.

The idea here is to leverage your money wisely and use your profits strategically to fund your growth, but without overextending yourself. In the example I mentioned earlier in the book—where we took on a big client and got into cash flow issues because their payments weren't coming in until three months later—we could have planned better.

My partners and I had taken some distributions out of the company around that time. But in hindsight, we should have left that money in to support the growth.

Cash flow gives you options. You can hire, expand, make improvements, take a vacation, or take distributions without harming the business.

Key Takeaway: Cash flow isn't just a metric; it's your safety net and your growth engine.

MAXIMIZING YOUR MARGINS

The main idea here is that you want to price for profit. Make sure your pricing reflects the value you're delivering.

Many business owners cringe at the thought of raising prices. But that's simply part of doing business. As you offer higher-quality products and services over time, and as your own expertise get sharper, you're offering more value.

Make sure to review all your prices at least annually (if not more frequently). Increasing prices is one of the easiest ways to make more money. Plus, your expenses are always going up, so your prices should too.

Let's look at it from the point of view of a consumer. If you subscribe to streaming services like Netflix, Disney Plus, Hulu, or Max, you are paying more for each of those today than you were two years ago.

Why? Because they have raised prices. Most people just accept those price hikes as a part of life and move on. Some people will cancel if price hikes are too drastic, and they don't perceive additional value. But most people just keep on paying whatever those companies charge.

It's natural to worry that raising prices will cost you customers. The truth is that worry is usually unfounded. It's important to continue to raise your prices to maintain profitability, and also to ensure you can still offer high quality to your customers or clients.

Once you do that, then you want to focus on high-margin activities. It goes back to the 80/20 Rule. Which 20 percent of your products and services are giving you 80 percent of your revenue?

Make sure to look at every measure of profitability across the board. Look at each segment of your business to make sure it's pulling its weight. Just like Starbucks, you might have verticals or product lines that are not serving you. Don't be afraid to get rid of those if they're not profitable.

Key Takeaway: Profitability requires cutting costs and raising prices, which will align your business with what delivers the most value.

✿ ✿ ✿

It may feel a little redundant to say this because we have talked about profitability from so many angles in this book. However, it bears repeating that profitability isn't just about having more money—it's about creating flexibility, stability, and options.

When you uncover hidden profits, master your cash flow, and focus on margins, you can turn your business into a powerful engine for freedom.

We're almost there! Now that we've worked through the first six elements of the Freedom Flywheel, we're ready to tackle the seventh and final one: Multiply Your Value.

Everything has led up to this moment. Turn the page to Chapter Eight to keep going!

Multiply
Your Value

MULTIPLY YOUR VALUE

We're at the final, but arguably most important, part of the Freedom Flywheel journey. If your business was selling your house, this would be a conversation about curb appeal. The key idea of multiplying your value is to create a business that buyers will fall all over themselves to purchase from you.

It means positioning your business as a scalable, attractive asset. People who buy a business are looking to buy an asset. They're not looking to buy a liability or a really expensive job.

Whether you want to sell your business or keep running it, it's important to keep increasing your business's value as the owner. It doesn't matter if you plan on passing it on to your kids, you think you might sell it to some high-level employees, or you're planning on an outside buyer.

Whatever the eventual outcome—and whoever the eventual owner—the most important high-level task you have as a business owner is increasing its value because multiplying its value gives you options.

Most business owners are basing their entire retirement plan on the value of their business. And most financial planners will assign some sort of value to your business based on what you've told them about it, even if it isn't accurate. They will not only be making decisions about how much money you need to retire, they will also be making decisions about your whole investment strategy based on that chunk of money represented by your business. If they believe that money in your business is super secure, they might take more risk with the rest of your portfolio.

There are all sorts of reasons to put as much effort as you can toward multiplying your business's value.

To that end, in this chapter we will look at three strategies for doing that: *focusing on value drivers, building a business buyers want*, and *giving yourself options*.

FOCUS ON VALUE DRIVERS

There are many ways to drive the value of your business. We've already talked about leadership depth, along with the importance of systems and processes to support your growth strategy and allow scalability.

Leadership depth matters because the buyer will want to know the business isn't going to fall apart once you're gone. Well-documented systems ensure the business can run efficiently and not create problems down the road. No potential buyer wants to buy a bunch of headaches.

Let's focus on another vital piece driving value: stable, predictable revenue streams.

A business can have various types of revenue. One of these is what I call "hunted" revenue, basically meaning one-off transactions. This type of revenue requires you to continuously find new customers, and it's also unpredictable and less valuable to buyers. Since there is no guarantee of repeat business, this is generally the least attractive type of revenue.

There are two other types that can radically change your profitability: reoccurring revenue and recurring revenue. They sound similar but are different.

Reoccurring revenue refers to repeat purchases from customers on an irregular schedule, such as event-based or seasonal transactions. This income is somewhat predictable and gives a business some stability.

On the other hand, **recurring revenue** means steady, predictable income from the same customers due to products like subscription services or maintenance contracts. This kind of revenue increases customer retention and loyalty, improves your cash flow, and also happens to be extremely attractive to a potential buyer of your business!

It shouldn't be any surprise that so many purchases have turned into subscription services. It seems like every app or cloud-based service comes with a monthly subscription. It's a great model for businesses and also provides a lot of benefits for customers who can count on updated apps and up-to-date service.

You can think of recurring revenue as the annuity that potential buyers are willing to pay a premium for.

A lot of business owners who have never considered recurring revenue are hesitant to jump into that game. But if you're creative, there are all kinds of ways you can implement this revenue model into your business, especially if you're a service-based business.

Key Takeaway: When a potential buyer is considering your business, they're not looking for headaches—they're looking for a great potential income source. And they're willing to pay more for a business with leadership depth, proven growth strategies, scalable systems, and recurring revenue.

BUILD A BUSINESS BUYERS WANT

When you think about your business from a buyer's perspective, you want to get rid of red flags. These are any risks that could scare off buyers. To go back to the analogy of selling your house, it would be like the buyer pointing out your leaky roof, peeling paint, and the weird smell you've gotten used to.

For your business, one such red flag might be customer concentration. They will ask for your top ten customers, and what percentage of your income comes from those ten. They'll also ask about legal issues like pending or past lawsuits.

You need to have very clean financials, preferably with at least five years of well-documented records. If you think you might sell in five years, you can start working on that now.

The sooner you start working on these things, the easier it will be to sell your business later on. Lots of business owners talk about the nightmare of going through due diligence when selling their business. But it's only a nightmare if you aren't prepared.

If you go through the steps of the Freedom Flywheel, you will be prepared to sell if and when the time comes. You'll already have everything in place. You're basically setting it up as you go.

Back to the main point: You want to eliminate red flags. The fewer headaches a potential buyer sees, the more likely they'll be to pay more. Nobody wants to pay for aggravation.

If you've ever sold your house, you know the pain of trying to fix all those lingering repairs you should have done over the years. You could have saved yourself a lot of heartache if you'd kept up with them.

Business owners are no different. It's easy to let things slide for another six months, a year, or five years because there is no urgency. Then all of a sudden, when you want to sell, you're in panic mode because there's a mountain of work to do.

The other advantage is that if you do this work as you go, you have a much better idea of what you're selling. Why? Because you'll know your business much better. You'll be familiar with every nook and cranny of it.

Going through this process can also give you the opportunity to enhance your brand. A strong brand identity makes your business more desirable. If you have a great reputation and your customers like you, that's a recipe for success. Your business can look great on paper, but you can't fake customer enthusiasm.

All this will also give your business more "curb appeal."

If you've had a growth plan before and you can document that it was successful, that's great. But even if you don't have the energy or desire to grow or scale, if you're well-positioned and can show the potential is there, buyers will love it.

Older business owners may not want to grow or scale, but the younger buyer will love having a plan to follow so that they can. If you can set up your business to appeal to more potential buyers, all the better!

Key Takeaway: Buyers aren't just looking for a business; they're looking for a great opportunity.

GIVE YOURSELF OPTIONS

We've spent a lot of time in this book talking about how to create value for others. But let's not neglect the importance of creating value for you as the owner.

Just like having cash flow gives you options, having a valuable business, built in the way I've described it in this book, gives you options as well.

The idea is that you want to build for freedom both now and in the future. Why? Because a business that's fun to run and highly profitable right *now* is going to be easy to sell and step away from *later*. You always want to have the option of continuing to own it *or* sell it. That way you're in control.

Even if you're not planning to sell anytime soon, you'll want to consider what a potential buyer might want so you can keep your options open. This is similar to building a house with the right number of bedrooms for its *future* buyer in mind.

It's very hard to time the sale of your business for optimal market conditions because they change all the time. But if you're creating value now, you can continue to scale, sell later, or do whatever you want. You simply have more options.

That's why I encourage you to always think like a buyer.

> ### A BUSINESS A BUYER WOULD WANT IS A BUSINESS YOU MIGHT WANT TO KEEP!

A potential buyer will look at your business objectively. Even though you're working in your business day to day, if you follow the principles I've laid out here, you'll be much better equipped to look at your business like a buyer would.

Key Takeaway: The more value you create, the more options you have for selling, scaling, or continuing to enjoy owning your business.

✿ ✿ ✿

As we look toward the end of our journey together, keep this in mind: A valuable business is about numbers and creating something buyers want, while ensuring it can thrive without you.

By focusing on value drivers, while creating a business buyers want, you're not just giving yourself options—you're building freedom. Which is what the journey is about.

Now that you've experienced the whole Freedom Flywheel, in the final chapter I want to challenge you to take action on this material.

It's one thing to read about concepts and understand them. But truly successful business owners don't just learn—they implement and execute. I can't wait to show you the next steps to continue your journey to freedom—whatever that means to you!

ARE YOU
READY TO FLY?

If you were born before the year 2000, you probably have fond memories of playing the classic *Mouse Trap* board game.

The goal of the game was to collect six pieces of "cheese" (cardboard cheese, of course). But the real fun of the game came when it was your turn to pull back the red lever to set the steel marble in motion.

A player turns a crank, turning gears and pushing on a red lever. The lever knocks a stop sign into a green shoe, which kicks a small bucket holding a metal ball. The ball rolls down some blue stairs and into a rain gutter, and then follows the gutter to bump into the bottom of a vertical rod. The top of the rod has a "helping hand" that bumps a bowling ball, making it fall through a "thing-a-ma-jig" and into a red bathtub, then out of the bathtub and onto a diving board. This catapults a green diver into a washtub, knocking loose a cage suspended from the top of a bumpy rod. The cage rattles down the rod and (hopefully) onto another player's unsuspecting mouse, trapping it. (Notwithstanding the fact that the mouse was made of plastic and not a sentient being in the first place. But I digress.)

Collecting the cheese pieces was just an excuse to watch all these crazy pieces come together to create something fun. So fun, in fact, that the *Mouse Trap* game is now over sixty years old and still a top seller for Hasbro.

Here's the thing, though: the fun of *Mouse Trap* doesn't come automatically. You have to set up the game first.

If you just dump out the pieces onto the floor, they're not going to magically arrange themselves on the board. You have to follow the directions and make sure it's all set up the way the designer intended.

Sure, it takes a bit of time to set up. But once it's ready, then the real fun can begin.

In the same way, the Freedom Flywheel takes some time to set up, but the results are well worth it! It creates that same kind of momentum, setting off a chain reaction of profitability, scalability, and greater potential than you can imagine.

In this book, you have learned how to create FREEDOM by implementing the key components of the Flywheel:

- **F**ix the Fires
- **R**everse Engineer Your Plan
- **E**mbrace Metrics That Matter
- **E**stablish Owner Independence
- **D**rive Growth and Scalability
- **O**ptimize Profitability
- **M**ultiply Your Value

I've done my best to make the Freedom Flywheel as simple and streamlined as possible by focusing on these seven elements.

As we talked about earlier in the book, a flywheel is a mechanical device that's designed to store energy and create momentum. When you apply this concept to the world of business, it's a collection of interdependent elements that work together in a system to create momentum, power, and success.

When you integrate the concepts of the Freedom Flywheel into *your* business, you get far more momentum, efficiency, profitability, and—perhaps most importantly—FUN!

I don't want your journey to end here at the end of this book. In fact, this is only the beginning! I want to invite you to work with me to put these principles into practice and start seeing amazing results.

FREEDOM IS WORTH IT

As a veterinarian, I've seen what happens when potential is wasted. A horse bred to win races can't succeed if it doesn't get the care and training it needs.

The same is true for your business. Without the right systems and strategy, it's easy to fall short of what's possible.

Making big changes in your business will never feel convenient. Life is always busy, and there will always be a reason to put it off. But the longer you wait, the harder it gets to catch up.

It's easy to think, *I'll fix this later*, but "later" rarely shows up when we expect it to. Instead of waiting, what if you started taking action today? When you do, you'll not just be investing in your business—you'll be investing in your future self.

Today I encourage you to consider what your future could be like a few years down the road. Do you want to own a booming, profitable business, knowing you made the changes that were needed? Or do you want to be weighed down by the regret that you didn't take action when you had the opportunity?

> **THERE'S NEVER A GOOD TIME TO MAKE CHANGES. LIFE GETS IN THE WAY. WE'RE BUSY. THERE'S ALWAYS TOO MUCH ON OUR PLATE.**

But as the old saying goes, the best time to plant a tree was twenty years ago. The second-best time is *today*.

Imagine a life where your business runs like a well-oiled machine, your team thrives, and you have the time and energy to focus on what matters most. That's what the Freedom Flywheel can give you.

When you implement the Freedom Flywheel, you're not just putting business systems in place. You're creating the life you truly want.

I've been where you are—busy, over-committed, and wondering if things would ever change. I'm living proof that they can. I've walked down this path myself, and I love helping others walk it too.

Now it's *your* turn.

I can understand if you are feeling a little overwhelmed. It's true that each of these steps can be daunting. You don't have to do it alone. The most successful business owners know when to ask for help—and that's where I come in.

Are you ready to stop being owned by your business and start owning your future? We can get started on your journey today, together.

Let's have a conversation to see if we're a great fit.

If you've made it this far, you already have the tools to transform your business. But let's not stop here. Transformation happens when you take action.

I want to personally invite you to work with me to implement the Freedom Flywheel in your business. Together, we can fast-track your results and create the freedom you deserve.

Visit ProductivePressure.com/Flywheel to connect with me and get this book's bonuses.

WOULD YOU REVIEW THIS BOOK?

If you enjoyed reading *The Business Owner's Freedom Flywheel*, would you kindly take a few moments to leave a review wherever you purchased it (and perhaps even Goodreads.com)? I'm grateful for your support. Thank you!

GRATITUDE

Writing a book is a little like running a business—you think you're in charge, but really, you're only as strong as the people around you. I've had an incredible team of supporters, encouragers, and idea-bouncers who have made this book (and quite frankly, my life) infinitely better.

First and foremost, to my husband Bob—thank you for always believing in me, no matter how many squirrels and shiny things I chase. Seriously, if I woke up tomorrow and decided to start an alpaca farm on Mars, you'd probably just nod, ask how you can help, and remind me to bring a good coat.

To my kids—Jack, for always making time to talk through my latest ideas and then dropping those sharp insights that make me go, "Why didn't I think of that?" And Emma, for your laser-focused attention to detail and willingness to slog through pages of my ramblings to give feedback that makes my thoughts make sense on paper. You two are the best volunteer editors ever!

To my clients—working with you has shown me that while these concepts might seem simple, they're far from easy. Your willingness to answer the tough questions, do the hard things, and make shit happen is what made me realize: This stuff matters. It's hard to see your own blind spots, and even harder to admit when you need help. That's why this framework exists—not to judge, but to give you a roadmap from where you are now to where you actually want to be. Thank you for trusting me to help you on that journey.

And finally, to my rockstar book team—Honorée Corder, Kent Sanders, MJ James, Alyssa Archer, Mike McConnell, and Dino Marino. You took on all the things so I didn't have to, which meant I could stay in my lane, do what I do best, and leave the rest to the pros. This book exists because of your expertise, patience, and ability to see the method to my madness.

To everyone who has supported, encouraged, or even just listened to me ramble about business strategy at inappropriate times—thank you. This book is for you.

ABOUT THE AUTHOR

Dawn Bloomer is a Business & Exit Planning Strategist who helps entrepreneurs build businesses that are fun to run now and easy to sell later. A former veterinarian-turned-business advisor, Dawn has been on both sides of the buyer-seller equation—and learned a lot along the way.

She bought into a well-established business, convinced she could make it better (despite having zero formal business training at the time). Years (and many wins and losses) later, she and her partner merged their practice into a larger group. From there, Dawn helped identify other businesses to buy to expand that group—until they were ultimately acquired by a much larger, private equity backed, aggregator. Along the way, she experienced firsthand the pain of due diligence, the challenges of post-transaction transitions, and the hard lessons that come from doing things the wrong way before figuring out how to do them right.

Now, as a Certified Exit Planning Advisor (CEPA) and MBA, Dawn helps business owners avoid the common pitfalls she's seen (and lived). She knows that building a business that runs smoothly without the owner at the center isn't always easy—it takes the right structure, strategy, and mindset—not to mention, hard work. That's why she created the Freedom Flywheel™ framework—to help business owners do it faster, with fewer headaches, and more clarity so they can have fun and freedom now, not just later.

When she's not helping business owners unlock the value in their companies, Dawn can be found having fun with her family, traveling, sailing, or pursuing another technology rabbit hole!

For more insights and resources, visit www.productivepressure.com or connect with Dawn on LinkedIn.